Praying the Rosary with the Bible Scriptures

Contents

How to use this book?

Our Lady has always emphasised the importance of the Holy Rosary prayer throughout the centuries. She tirelessly reminds us of its power in many apparitions, including Fatima and Medjugorje, which in the latter still continues to happen to the present day.

The purpose of this book is to help you, dear reader to meditate on each mystery with a support of the Bible scriptures. At the bottom of each gospel extract you will find guiding tips on how to reflect on each decade of the rosary.

May the Beads of Our Lady bring peace, healing, love and the blessings from the purest hands of the Mediatrix of all graces.

"Continue to pray the Rosary every day."
Our Lady of Fatima to Sister Lucia

The 15 Promises of the Rosary

1. Those who faithfully serve me by the recitation of the Rosary shall receive signal graces.

2. I promise my special protection and the greatest graces to all those who shall recite the Rosary.

3. The Rosary shall be a powerful armor against hell. It will destroy vice, decrease sin, and defeat heresies.

4. The recitation of the Rosary will cause virtue and good works to flourish. It will obtain for souls the abundant mercy of God. It will withdraw the hearts of men from the love of the world and its vanities, and will lift them to the desire of eternal things. Oh, that souls would sanctify themselves by this means.

5. The soul which recommends itself to me by the recitation of the Rosary shall not perish.

6. Those who recite my Rosary devoutly, applying themselves to the consideration of its sacred mysteries, shall never be conquered by misfortune. In His justice, God will not chastise them; nor shall they perish by an unprovided death, i.e., be unprepared for heaven. Sinners shall convert. The just shall persevere in grace and become worthy of eternal life.

7. Those who have a true devotion to the Rosary shall not die without the sacraments of the Church.

8. Those who faithfully recite the Rosary shall have, during their life and at their death, the light of God and the plenitude of His graces. At the moment of death, they shall participate in the merits of the saints in paradise.

9. I shall deliver from purgatory those who have been devoted to the Rosary.

10. The faithful children of the Rosary shall merit a high degree of glory in heaven.

11. By the recitation of the Rosary you shall obtain all that you ask of me.

12. Those who propagate the holy Rosary shall be aided by me in their necessities.

13. I have obtained from my Divine Son that all the advocates of the Rosary shall have for intercessors the entire celestial court during their life and at the hour of their death.

14. All who recite the Rosary are my beloved children and the brothers and sisters of my only Son, Jesus Christ.

15. Devotion for my Rosary is a great sign of predestination.

Blessed Virgin Mary revealed the promises to blessed Alanus de la Roche, known as Alan Rupe, a dominican monk in 1464.

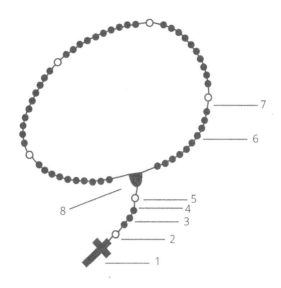

1. Start with making the sign Cross and pray the **'Apostles Creed'**
2. Say the **'Our Father'**
3. Say the **'Hail Mary'** 3 times
4. Say the **'Glory Be'**
5. Announce the First Mystery and pray **'Our Father'**
6. Say **'Hail Mary'** 10 times and
7. Conclude the Mystery with **'Glory Be'** and **'Oh my Jesus'.** Repeat steps 1 - 6 with the next following Mysteries.
8. Say the 'Hail holy Queen' at the end of the Rosary.

It is suggested to add the following prayers: 'Angel of God', 'St. Michael Archangel' and 'To you oh blessed Joseph' at the end of the Rosary.

Joyful Mysteries- Mondays and Saturdays
Sorrowful Mysteries - Tuesdays and Fridays
Luminous Mysteries - Thursdays
Glorious Mysteries - Wednesdays and Sundays

Rosary Prayers

The Sign of the Cross

The Apostles' Creed

I believe in God,
the Father Almighty,
Creator of heaven and earth,
and in Jesus Christ, His only Son, our Lord,
who was conceived by the Holy Spirit,
born of the Virgin Mary,
suffered under Pontius Pilate,
was crucified, died and was buried;
He descended into hell;
on the third day He rose again from the dead;
He ascended into heaven,
and is seated at the right hand of God the Father
Almighty;
from there He will come to judge the living and the
dead.
I believe in the Holy Spirit,
the Holy Catholic Church,
the communion of Saints,
the forgiveness of sins,
the resurrection of the body,
and life everlasting.
Amen.

Our Father

Our Father, Who art in Heaven, hallowed be Thy name; Thy Kingdom come, Thy will be done on earth as it is in Heaven. Give us this day our daily bread; and forgive us our trespasses as we forgive those who trespass against us; and lead us not into temptation, but deliver us from evil. Amen.

Hail Mary

Hail Mary full of Grace, the Lord is with thee.
Blessed are thou amongst women and blessed is the fruit of thy womb Jesus.
Holy Mary Mother of God,
pray for us sinners now and at the hour of our death. Amen.

Glory Be

Glory be to the Father and to the Son and to the Holy Spirit. As it was in the beginning is now, and ever shall be, world without end. Amen.

Oh my Jesus (Or Lady asked in Fatima to say this prayer)after each decade)
O my Jesus, forgive us our sins,
save us from the fires of hell;
lead all souls to heaven especially those who are in most need of
Your mercy.
Amen.

Concluding Prayers

Hail Holy Queen

Hail, holy Queen, mother of mercy, our life, our sweetness, and our hope. To thee do we cry, poor banished children of Eve. Turn then, most gracious advocate, thine eyes of mercy toward us, and after this our exile show us the blessed fruit of thy womb, Jesus. O clement, O loving, O sweet Virgin Mary. Amen.

To You oh Blessed Joseph

To you, O blessed Joseph,
do we come in our tribulation,
and having implored the help of your most holy Spouse, we confidently invoke your patronage also.
Through that charity which bound you to the Immaculate Virgin Mother of God and through the paternal love with which you embraced the Child Jesus, we humbly beg you graciously to regard the inheritance which Jesus Christ has purchased by his Blood, and with your power and strength to aid us in our necessities.
O most watchful guardian of the Holy Family, defend the chosen children of Jesus Christ;
O most loving father, ward off from us every contagion of error and corrupting influence;

O our most mighty protector, be kind to us
and from heaven assist us in our struggle
with the power of darkness.
As once you rescued the Child Jesus from deadly peril,
so now protect God's Holy Church from the snares of
the enemy and from all adversity; shield, too, each
one of us by your constant protection, so that,
supported by your example and your aid, we may be
able to live piously, to die in holiness, and to obtain
eternal happiness in heaven. Amen.

V. Pray for us, O holy Mother of God.
R. That we may be made worthy of the promises of
Christ.

O GOD, WHOSE only-begotten Son by His life, death
and resurrection, has purchased for us the rewards of
eternal life; grant, we beseech Thee, that by
meditating upon these mysteries of the Most Holy
Rosary of the Blessed Virgin Mary, we may imitate
what they contain and obtain what they promise,
through the same Christ our Lord. Amen.

Joyful Mysteries

1. The Annunciation of the Lord to Mary

In the sixth month of Elizabeth's pregnancy, God sent the angel Gabriel to Nazareth, a town in Galilee, to a virgin pledged to be married to a man named Joseph, a descendant of David. The virgin's name was Mary. The angel went to her and said, "Greetings, you who are highly favored! The Lord is with you."

Mary was greatly troubled at his words and wondered what kind of greeting this might be. But the angel said to her, "Do not be afraid, Mary; you have found favor with God. You will conceive and give birth to a son, and you are to call him Jesus. He will be great and will be called the Son of the Most High. The Lord God will give him the throne of his father David, and he will reign over Jacob's descendants forever; his kingdom will never end."

"How will this be," Mary asked the angel, "since I am a virgin?"

The angel answered, "The Holy Spirit will come on you, and the power of the Most High will overshadow you. So the holy one to be born will be called the Son of God. Even Elizabeth your relative is going to have a child in her old age, and she who was said to be unable to conceive is in her sixth month. For no word from God will ever fail."

"I am the Lord's servant," Mary answered. "May your word to me be fulfilled." Then the angel left her.

(Luke 1, 26 - 38)

Meditiatio

Read the Bible verses several times. Let them slowly sink into your mind and spirit. Try to understand what the Lord is telling you through this passage. Which verse spoke to you most?

Oratio

Now it's your turn to speak to God. Open your heart before Him. Pray with simplicity and spontaneously.

Contemplatio

Be still before the Lord. Contemplate this quiet and peaceful time in His presence, allowing Holy Spirit to work within you.

Our Father ...
Hail Mary ... (x10)
Glory be ...
Oh my Jesus...

2. Visitation

At that time Mary got ready and hurried to a town in the hill country of Judea, where she entered Zechariah's home and greeted Elizabeth. When Elizabeth heard Mary's greeting, the baby leaped in her womb, and Elizabeth was filled with the Holy Spirit. In a loud voice she exclaimed: "Blessed are you among women, and blessed is the child you will bear! But why am I so favored, that the mother of my Lord should come to me? As soon as the sound of your greeting reached my ears, the baby in my womb leaped for joy. Blessed is she who has believed that the Lord would fulfill his promises to her!"

(Luke 1, 39 -45)

Meditiatio

Read the Bible verses several times. Let them slowly sink into your mind and spirit. Try to understand what the Lord is telling you through this passage. Which verse spoke to you most?

Oratio

Now it's your turn to speak to God. Open your heart before Him. Pray with simplicity and spontaneously.

Contemplatio

Be still before the Lord. Contemplate this quiet and peaceful time in His presence, allowing Holy Spirit to work within you.

Our Father ...
Hail Mary ... (x10)
Glory be ...
Oh my Jesus...

3. The Nativity of Jesus in Bethlehem

And so it was, that, while they were there, the days were accomplished that she should be delivered. And she brought forth her firstborn son, and wrapped Him in swaddling clothes, and laid Him in a manger; because there was no room for them in the inn. And there were in the same country shepherds abiding in the field, keeping watch over their flock by night. And, lo, the angel of the Lord came upon them, and the glory of the Lord shone round about them: and they were sore afraid. And the angel said unto them: "Fear not: for, behold, I bring you good tidings of great joy, which shall be to all people. For unto you is born this day in the city of David a Saviour, which is Christ the Lord. And this shall be a sign unto you; Ye shall find the babe wrapped in swaddling clothes, lying in a manger".

(Luke 2,6-12)

Meditiatio

Read the Bible verses several times. Let them slowly sink into your mind and spirit. Try to understand what the Lord is telling you through this passage. Which verse spoke to you most?

Oratio

Now it's your turn to speak to God. Open your heart before Him. Pray with simplicity and spontaneously.

Contemplatio

Be still before the Lord. Contemplate this quiet and peaceful time in His presence, allowing Holy Spirit to work within you.

Our Father ...
Hail Mary ... (x10)
Glory be ...
Oh my Jesus...

4. The Presentation of Jesus to the Temple

And when the days of her purification according to the law of Moses were accomplished, they brought Him to Jerusalem, to present Him to the Lord; And to offer a sacrifice according to that which is said in the law of the Lord, A pair of turtledoves, or two young pigeons. And, behold, there was a man in Jerusalem, whose name was Simeon; and the same man was just and devout, waiting for the consolation of Israel: and the Holy Ghost was upon Him. ...When the parents brought in the child Jesus, to do for Him after the custom of the law, Then took he Him up in His arms, and blessed God, and said: "Lord, now lettest thou thy servant depart in peace, according to thy word: For mine eyes have seen thy salvation... A light to lighten the Gentiles, and the glory of thy people Israel." And Joseph and His mother marvelled at those things which were spoken of Him. And Simeon blessed them, and said unto Mary His mother: "Behold, this child is set for the fall and rising again of many in Israel; and for a sign which shall be spoken against; (Yea, a sword shall pierce through thy own soul also,) that the thoughts of many hearts may be revealed."

(Luke 2,22-35)

Meditiatio

Read the Bible verses several times. Let them slowly sink into your mind and spirit. Try to understand what the Lord is telling you through this passage. Which verse spoke to you most?

Oratio

Now it's your turn to speak to God. Open your heart before Him. Pray with simplicity and spontaneously.

Contemplatio

Be still before the Lord. Contemplate this quiet and peaceful time in His presence, allowing Holy Spirit to work within you.

Our Father ...
Hail Mary ... (x10)
Glory be ...
Oh my Jesus...

5. The Finding of Jesus in the Temple

When they were on their way home after the feast, the boy Jesus stayed behind in Jerusalem without his parents knowing it.

They assumed he was with the caravan, and it was only after a day's journey that they went to look for him among their relations and acquaintances. When they failed to find him they went back to Jerusalem looking for him everywhere. Three days later, they found him in the Temple, sitting among the doctors, listening to them, and asking them questions; and all those who heard him were astounded at his intelligence and his replies. They were overcome when they saw him, and his mother said to him, 'My child, why have, you done this to us? See how worried your father and I have been, looking for you.'

'Why were you looking for me?' he replied 'Did you not know that I must be busy with my Father's affairs?' But they did not understand what he meant.

The hidden life at Nazareth resumed. He then went down with them and came to Nazareth and lived under their authority. His mother stored up all these things in her heart.

(Luke 2, 43-51)

Meditiatio

Read the Bible verses several times. Let them slowly sink into your mind and spirit. Try to understand what the Lord is telling you through this passage. Which verse spoke to you most?

Oratio

Now it's your turn to speak to God. Open your heart before Him. Pray with simplicity and spontaneously.

Contemplatio

Be still before the Lord. Contemplate this quiet and peaceful time in His presence, allowing Holy Spirit to work within you.

Our Father ...
Hail Mary ... (x10)
Glory be ...
Oh my Jesus...

Sorrowful Mysteries

1. The Agony of Jesus in the Garden

In his anguish he prayed more earnestly, and his sweat became like great drops of blood falling down on the ground. When he got up from prayer, he came to the disciples and found them sleeping because of grief, and he said to them, "Why are you sleeping? Get up and pray that you may not come into the time of trial."

(Luke 22, 44-46)

Meditiatio

Read the Bible verses several times. Let them slowly sink into your mind and spirit. Try to understand what the Lord is telling you through this passage. Which verse spoke to you most?

Oratio

Now it's your turn to speak to God. Open your heart before Him. Pray with simplicity and spontaneously.

Contemplatio

Be still before the Lord. Contemplate this quiet and peaceful time in His presence, allowing Holy Spirit to work within you.

Our Father ...
Hail Mary ... (x10)
Glory be ...
Oh my Jesus...

2. The Scourging of Jesus at the Pillar

They struck his head with a reed, spat upon him, and knelt down in homage to him. 20 After mocking him, they stripped him of the purple cloak and put his own clothes on him. Then they led him out to crucify him.

Mk 15, 19-20

Meditiatio

Read the Bible verses several times. Let them slowly sink into your mind and spirit. Try to understand what the Lord is telling you through this passage. Which verse spoke to you most?

Oratio

Now it's your turn to speak to God. Open your heart before Him. Pray with simplicity and spontaneously.

Contemplatio

Be still before the Lord. Contemplate this quiet and peaceful time in His presence, allowing Holy Spirit to work within you.

Our Father ...
Hail Mary ... (x10)
Glory be ...
Oh my Jesus...

3. The Crowning with Thorns

Then the soldiers led Jesus away inside the palace, that is, the Praetorium, and they called the whole cohort together. 17 They dressed him in a purple robe and after twisting some thorns into a crown, they placed it on him. 18 Then they began to salute him with the words, "Hail, King of the Jews!" 19 They repeatedly struck his head with a reed, spat upon him, and knelt down before him in homage. 20 And when they had finished mocking him, they stripped him of his purple robe and dressed him in his own clothes. Then they led him out to crucify him.

Mk 15, 16-20

Meditiatio

Read the Bible verses several times. Let them slowly sink into your mind and spirit. Try to understand what the Lord is telling you through this passage. Which verse spoke to you most?

Oratio

Now it's your turn to speak to God. Open your heart before Him. Pray with simplicity and spontaneously.

Contemplatio

Be still before the Lord. Contemplate this quiet and peaceful time in His presence, allowing Holy Spirit to work within you.

Our Father ...
Hail Mary ... (x10)
Glory be ...
Oh my Jesus...

4. Carrying of the Cross

As they were leading Him away they seized on a man, Simon from Cyrene, who was coming in from the country, and made Him shoulder the cross and carry it behind Jesus. Large numbers of people followed Him, and women too, who mourned and lamented for Him. But Jesus turned to them and said, 'Daughters of Jerusalem, do not weep for me; weep rather for yourselves and for your children. For look, the days are surely coming when people will say, "Blessed are those who are barren, the wombs that have never borne children, the breasts that have never suckled!" Then they will begin to say to the mountains, "Fall on us!"; to the hills, "Cover us!" For if this is what is done to green wood, what will be done when the wood is dry?' Now they were also leading out two others, criminals, to be executed with Him.

(Luke 23,26-32)

Meditiatio

Read the Bible verses several times. Let them slowly sink into your mind and spirit. Try to understand what the Lord is telling you through this passage. Which verse spoke to you most?

Oratio

Now it's your turn to speak to God. Open your heart before Him. Pray with simplicity and spontaneously.

Contemplatio

Be still before the Lord. Contemplate this quiet and peaceful time in His presence, allowing Holy Spirit to work within you.

Our Father ...
Hail Mary ... (x10)
Glory be ...
Oh my Jesus...

5. The Crucifixion and Death of Jesus

After this, Jesus knew that everything had now been completed, and to fulfil the scripture perfectly he said: 'I am thirsty'. A jar-full of vinegar stood there, so putting a sponge soaked in the vinegar on a hyssop stick they held it up to his mouth. After Jesus had taken the vinegar he said, 'It is accomplished'; and bowing his head he gave up his spirit.

(John 19, 28-30)

Meditiatio

Read the Bible verses several times. Let them slowly sink into your mind and spirit. Try to understand what the Lord is telling you through this passage. Which verse spoke to you most?

Oratio

Now it's your turn to speak to God. Open your heart before Him. Pray with simplicity and spontaneously.

Contemplatio

Be still before the Lord. Contemplate this quiet and peaceful time in His presence, allowing Holy Spirit to work within you.

Our Father ...
Hail Mary ... (x10)
Glory be ...
Oh my Jesus...

Light Mysteries

1. The Baptism of Jesus

Then Jesus appeared: he came from Galilee to the Jordan to be baptised by John. John tried to dissuade him. 'It is I who need baptism from you' he said 'and yet you come to me!' But Jesus replied, 'Leave it like this for the time being; it is fitting that we should, in this way, do all that righteousness demands'. At this, John gave in to him. As soon as Jesus was baptised he came up from the water, and suddenly the heavens opened and he saw the Spirit of God descending like a dove and coming down on him. And a voice spoke from heaven, 'This is my Son, the Beloved; my favour rests on him'.

(Mt 3, 13-17)

Meditiatio

Read the Bible verses several times. Let them slowly sink into your mind and spirit. Try to understand what the Lord is telling you through this passage. Which verse spoke to you most?

Oratio

Now it's your turn to speak to God. Open your heart before Him. Pray with simplicity and spontaneously.

Contemplatio

Be still before the Lord. Contemplate this quiet and peaceful time in His presence, allowing Holy Spirit to work within you.

Our Father ...
Hail Mary ... (x10)
Glory be ...
Oh my Jesus...

2. The Wedding of Cana

Three days later there was a wedding at Cana in Galilee. The mother of Jesus was there, and Jesus and his disciples had also been invited. When they ran out of wine, since the wine provided for the wedding was all finished, the mother of Jesus said to him, 'They have no wine'. Jesus said 'Woman, why turn to me? My hour has not come yet.' His mother said to the servants, 'Do whatever he tells you'. There were six stone water jars standing there, meant for the ablutions that are customary among the Jews: each could hold twenty or thirty gallons. Jesus said to the servants, 'Fill the jars with water', and they filled them to the brim. 'Draw some out now' he told them 'and take it to the steward.' They did this; the steward tasted the water, and it had turned into wine. Having no idea where it came from – only the servants who had drawn the water knew – the steward called the bridegroom and said; 'People generally serve the best wine first, and keep the cheaper sort till the guests have had plenty to drink; but you have kept the best wine till now'.

(John 2, 1-12)

Meditiatio

Read the Bible verses several times. Let them slowly sink into your mind and spirit. Try to understand what the Lord is telling you through this passage. Which verse spoke to you most?

Oratio

Now it's your turn to speak to God. Open your heart before Him. Pray with simplicity and spontaneously.

Contemplatio

Be still before the Lord. Contemplate this quiet and peaceful time in His presence, allowing Holy Spirit to work within you.

Our Father ...
Hail Mary ... (x10)
Glory be ...
Oh my Jesus...

3. The Proclamation of the Kingdom of God

 Seeing the crowds, he went up the hill. There he sat down and was joined by his disciples. Then he began to speak. This is what he taught them: 'How happy are the poor in spirit; theirs is the kingdom of heaven.

(Mt, 5, 1-3)

Meditiatio

Read the Bible verses several times. Let them slowly sink into your mind and spirit. Try to understand what the Lord is telling you through this passage. Which verse spoke to you most?

Oratio

Now it's your turn to speak to God. Open your heart before Him. Pray with simplicity and spontaneously.

Contemplatio

Be still before the Lord. Contemplate this quiet and peaceful time in His presence, allowing Holy Spirit to work within you.

Our Father ...
Hail Mary ... (x10)
Glory be ...
Oh my Jesus...

4. The Transfiguration on Mount Tabor

Six days later, Jesus took with him Peter and James and John and led them up a high mountain where they could be alone by themselves. There in their presence he was transfigured: his clothes became dazzlingly white, whiter than any earthly bleacher could make them. Elijah appeared to them with Moses; and they were talking with Jesus. Then Peter spoke to Jesus: 'Rabbi,' he said 'it is wonderful for us to be here; so let us make three tents, one for you, one for Moses and one for Elijah'. He did not know what to say; they were so frightened. And a cloud came, covering them in shadow; and there came a voice from the cloud, 'This is my Son, the Beloved. Listen to him.'

(Mk 9, 2-7)

Meditiatio

Read the Bible verses several times. Let them slowly sink into your mind and spirit. Try to understand what the Lord is telling you through this passage. Which verse spoke to you most?

Oratio

Now it's your turn to speak to God. Open your heart before Him. Pray with simplicity and spontaneously.

Contemplatio

Be still before the Lord. Contemplate this quiet and peaceful time in His presence, allowing Holy Spirit to work within you.

Our Father ...
Hail Mary ... (x10)
Glory be ...
Oh my Jesus...

5. The Institution of the Eucharist

And as they were eating he took some bread, and when he had said the blessing he broke it and gave it to them. 'Take it,' he said 'this is my body.' Then he took a cup, and when he had returned thanks he gave it to them, and all drank from it, and he said to them, 'This is my blood, the blood of the covenant, which is to be poured out for many. I tell you solemnly, I shall not drink any more wine until the day I drink the new wine in the kingdom of God.'

(Mk 14, 22-25)

Meditiatio

Read the Bible verses several times. Let them slowly sink into your mind and spirit. Try to understand what the Lord is telling you through this passage. Which verse spoke to you most?

Oratio

Now it's your turn to speak to God. Open your heart before Him. Pray with simplicity and spontaneously.

Contemplatio

Be still before the Lord. Contemplate this quiet and peaceful time in His presence, allowing Holy Spirit to work within you.

Our Father ...
Hail Mary ... (x10)
Glory be ...
Oh my Jesus...

Glorious Mysteries

1. The Resurrection of Jesus Christ

On the first day of the week, at the first sign of dawn, they went to the tomb with the spices they had prepared. They found that the stone had been rolled away from the tomb, but on entering discovered that the body of the Lord Jesus was not there. As they stood there not knowing what to think, two men in brilliant clothes suddenly appeared at their side. Terrified, the women lowered their eyes. But the two men said to them, 'Why look among the dead for someone who is alive?

He is not here; he has risen. Remember what he told you when he was still in Galilee: that the Son of Man had to be handed over into the power of sinful men and be crucified, and rise again on the third day?'

And they remembered his words.

(Luke 24, 1-8)

Meditiatio

Read the Bible verses several times. Let them slowly sink into your mind and spirit. Try to understand what the Lord is telling you through this passage. Which verse spoke to you most?

Oratio

Now it's your turn to speak to God. Open your heart before Him. Pray with simplicity and spontaneously.

Contemplatio

Be still before the Lord. Contemplate this quiet and peaceful time in His presence, allowing Holy Spirit to work within you.

Our Father ...
Hail Mary ... (x10)
Glory be ...
Oh my Jesus...

2. The Ascension of Jesus Christ

Then he took them out as far as the outskirts of Bethany, and lifting up his hands he blessed them. Now as he blessed them, he withdrew from them and was carried up to heaven. They worshipped him and then went back to Jerusalem full of joy; and they were continually in the Temple praising God.

(Luke 24, 50-53)

Meditiatio

Read the Bible verses several times. Let them slowly sink into your mind and spirit. Try to understand what the Lord is telling you through this passage. Which verse spoke to you most?

Oratio

Now it's your turn to speak to God. Open your heart before Him. Pray with simplicity and spontaneously.

Contemplatio

Be still before the Lord. Contemplate this quiet and peaceful time in His presence, allowing Holy Spirit to work within you.

Our Father ...
Hail Mary ... (x10)
Glory be ...
Oh my Jesus...

3. The Descent of the Holy Ghost

When Pentecost day came round, they had all met in one room, when suddenly they heard what sounded like a powerful wind from heaven, the noise of which filled the entire house in which they were sitting; and something appeared to them that seemed like tongues of fire; these separated and came to rest on the head of each of them. They were all filled with the Holy Spirit, and began to speak foreign languages as the Spirit gave them the gift of speech.

(Acts 2, 1-4)

Meditiatio

Read the Bible verses several times. Let them slowly sink into your mind and spirit. Try to understand what the Lord is telling you through this passage. Which verse spoke to you most?

Oratio

Now it's your turn to speak to God. Open your heart before Him. Pray with simplicity and spontaneously.

Contemplatio

Be still before the Lord. Contemplate this quiet and peaceful time in His presence, allowing Holy Spirit to work within you.

Our Father ...
Hail Mary ... (x10)
Glory be ...
Oh my Jesus...

4. The Assumption of the Blessed Virgin Mary

Father, I want those you have given me to be with me where I am, so that they may always see the glory you have given me because you loved me before the foundation of the world.

(J 17, 24)

Meditiatio

Read the Bible verses several times. Let them slowly sink into your mind and spirit. Try to understand what the Lord is telling you through this passage. Which verse spoke to you most?

Oratio

Now it's your turn to speak to God. Open your heart before Him. Pray with simplicity and spontaneously.

Contemplatio

Be still before the Lord. Contemplate this quiet and peaceful time in His presence, allowing Holy Spirit to work within you.

Our Father ...
Hail Mary ... (x10)
Glory be ...
Oh my Jesus...

5. The Crowning of Our Lady the Queen of Heaven

Those who prove victorious I will allow to share my throne, just as I was victorious myself and took my place with my Father on his throne.

(Ap 3, 21)

Meditiatio

Read the Bible verses several times. Let them slowly sink into your mind and spirit. Try to understand what the Lord is telling you through this passage. Which verse spoke to you most?

Oratio

Now it's your turn to speak to God. Open your heart before Him. Pray with simplicity and spontaneously.

Contemplatio

Be still before the Lord. Contemplate this quiet and peaceful time in His presence, allowing Holy Spirit to work within you.

Our Father ...
Hail Mary ... (x10)
Glory be ...
Oh my Jesus...

Printed in Great Britain
by Amazon

30574723R00036